HOW THE INTERNET WORKS

BY JENNIFER SWANSON • ILLUSTRATED BY GLEN MULLALY

The Child's World

Published by The Child's World®
1980 Lookout Drive • Mankato, MN 56003-1705
800-599-READ • www.childsworld.com

ACKNOWLEDGMENTS
The Child's World®: Mary Berendes, Publishing Director
Content Consultant: Paul Ohmann, PhD, Associate Professor
    of Physics, University of St. Thomas
The Design Lab: Design and production
Red Line Editorial: Editorial direction

LIBRARY OF CONGRESS
CATALOGING-IN-PUBLICATION DATA
Swanson, Jennifer.
 How the internet works / by Jennifer Swanson;
illustrated by Glen Mullaly.
     p. cm.
 Includes bibliographical references and index.
 ISBN 978-1-60973-218-9 (library reinforced: alk. paper)
1. Internet—Juvenile literature. I. Mullaly, Glen, 1968– ill.
II. Title.
 TK5105.875.I57S925 2012
 004.678—dc22   2011010918

Photo Credits © Sean Locke/iStockphoto, cover, 1, 26 (top);
AP Images, 6, 28 (bottom right); Anthony Berger/Library
of Congress, 7; Library of Congress, 8, 26 (bottom left),
27 (bottom left); iStockphoto, 16, 25, 26 (bottom right),
29 (right); Shutterstock Images, 23, 27 (bottom right), 28
(bottom left); Jen Grantham/iStockphoto, 27 (top); Stephen
Coburn/Shutterstock Images, 28 (top); Tuomas Kujansuu/
iStockphoto, 29 (left)

Printed in the United States of America in Mankato,
Minnesota.
July 2011
PA02092

ABOUT THE AUTHOR
Jennifer Swanson's first love is science,
and she is thrilled to be able to combine
that with her passion for writing. She has
a bachelor of science in chemistry from
the US Naval Academy and a master of
science in education from Walden University.
Jennifer is currently employed as a middle
school science instructor for Johns Hopkins
University's Center for Talented Youth.

ABOUT THE ILLUSTRATOR
Glen Mullaly draws neato pictures for kids
of all ages from his swanky studio on the
west coast of Canada. He lives with his
awesomely understanding wife and their
spectacularly indifferent cat. Glen loves
old books, magazines, and cartoons, and
someday wants to illustrate a book on
How Monsters Work!

TABLE OF CONTENTS

CHAPTER ONE

BURSTING WITH NEWS

You've just gotten the best news. But who can you tell? It's 9:30 at night, and you're supposed to be asleep. You can't stop bouncing on the bed with excitement. You *will* burst if you don't tell someone.

You look around your room and spy your computer. The Internet! You can video chat with your friend across the country. It's three hours earlier there, so you know she's still up. You jump out of bed and turn on the computer.

In a couple seconds, your friend's face is smiling at you on the screen. A thousand miles between you turns into nothing with just a press of a key.

What was it like for your parents when they were bursting with news? What about your grandparents? Let's take a look back at how technology helped people connect 20, 50, or more than 500 years ago.

The World Wide Web was up and running by 1991. Now people could send more than just words over the Internet. The Web also let users jump easily from site to site by clicking on links. In 1993, the first browser came out, making the Web even easier to use. The Internet started to grow amazingly fast.

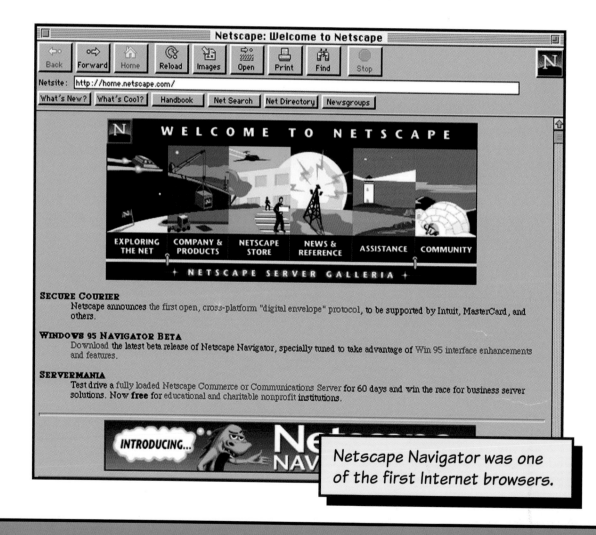

Netscape Navigator was one of the first Internet browsers.

The Internet was just taking shape. By the late 1960s, some government and university computers were connected in a **network** called ARPANET. This network had been started by the US Department of Defense as part of a military defense strategy. By 1981, more than 200 computers were linked, and ARPANET was split in two. Military computers formed one network. The other network grew into what we know as the Internet today.

Abraham Lincoln was the first president to set up a system to keep in contact with his generals during war. He used the best technology around at the time—the telegraph. President Lincoln's messages informed generals of urgent and important intelligence.

Abraham Lincoln in 1864

Johannes Gutenberg of Germany invented the printing press in 1440. Before this, books in Europe were written out by hand. Now, many books could be made at one time. This made the price of books go down, so more people could own them. Information could spread easily and to more people.

Gutenberg looking at the first paper off the printing press in 1440

The Internet crosses the planet and even reaches into space. At NASA's Web site, you can watch astronauts live at the International Space Station!

Smartphones, laptops, MP3 players, and e-readers can get to the Internet 24 hours a day. Articles, books, blogs, maps, videos, music—it's all available at the touch of your fingers.

Number of people in the United States in 2010: **310 million**

Number of people who use the Internet in the United States in 2010: **more than 240 million**

Number of people in the world in 2011: **almost 7 billion**

Number of people who use the Internet worldwide: **about 2 billion**

Number of people who use Facebook: **more than 500 million**

Number of videos viewed on YouTube every day: **more than 2 billion**

CHAPTER TWO

WHAT EXACTLY IS THE INTERNET?

The Internet is a network. It's a vast system that connects computers from all over the world. It can have wires or be wireless. Either way, all the computers inside it are able to share information.

Think of the Internet as a spider web. A huge, complicated web can stretch over a large space. Have you ever looked closely at a spider web? Not all the sticky threads are connected to the center. However, all the threads are still connected to each other.

The Internet doesn't have a center at all. Instead, tens of thousands of smaller networks are linked together. You can post whatever you want from your computer, and it can be seen by anyone on the whole network.

World Wide Wonderful

Did you know the Internet and the Web, or World Wide Web, are two different things? The Internet is a network. It simply sends information from one place to another. The Web is one way information is found on the Internet.

Think of it like this: The Internet is a highway. The Web is a car that takes you to the places you want to go. E-mails, photos, videos, and other information are the interesting stops along the way!

WEB WORDS

You're on your favorite Web site, and you scroll down the list of topics. Armchairs, blinkers, dingbats . . . Aha! You find your topic—gorillas—and see that it's highlighted blue. You click on it, and in seconds you're taken to another cool site.

That probably sounds familiar. But did you know that blue word has a term? It's called a hyperlink.

CHECK OUT THESE OTHER WEB WORDS:

Hypertext markup language, or HTML: This is the computer language used to make hyperlinks and format Web pages in general.

Uniform resource locator, or URL: This is basically a Web site's address. It's the text you type into the box at the top of the page to get to your favorite sites.

Browser: This is an application, such as Internet Explorer or Safari, that helps you move from site to site easily. It's like your tour bus through the Internet. It stops at an interesting place and lets you look around. Then you hop back onboard and—zip! It takes you to another cool spot.

Search engine: This is an application, like Google, that lets you type in key words to find what you're looking for on the Web.

CHAPTER THREE

SO MANY PATHS

This diagram shows three important types of hardware that make up the Internet:

Clients are computers or devices like yours that seek information.

Servers are computers that store and send the information you're looking for.

Routers direct the flow of traffic.

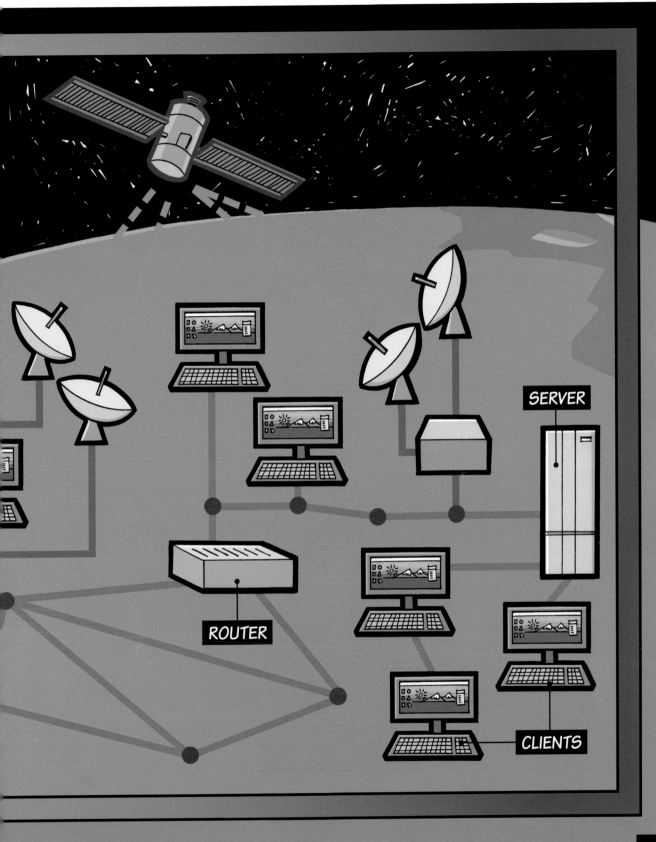

SERVER

ROUTER

CLIENTS

Between clients, servers, and routers, information can travel many paths—both on wires or through the air. Let's look at some of these roads:

1. Cable wires. These are the same cables that bring you cable TV.

2. Traditional copper phone lines. A DSL (digital subscriber line) connection can make these a lot faster than they used to be.

3. Fiber-optic cables. These special telephone lines are made of pure glass fibers as thin as human hairs. They can send and receive huge amounts of information as patterns of light.

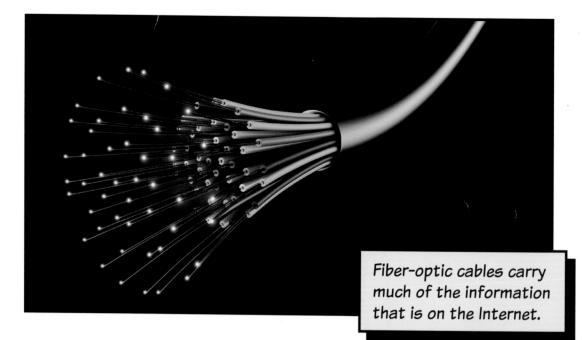

Fiber-optic cables carry much of the information that is on the Internet.

4. Radio waves. Satellites and cell phone towers send and receive information on radio waves zipping through the air.

MODEMS

The information in your computer is in digital form. Everything in there—photos, sounds, text—is in a numeric code. That code is made up of just 1s and 0s. But those 1s and 0s are strung together in patterns, like 11000011 or 1111000011010l. The possibilities are endless, so those patterns carry tons of information.

Say that information is a photo of your poodle Cha-Cha, and you want to e-mail it to your cousin. To get onto the Internet from your computer, Cha-Cha will likely have to travel over phone or cable wires. To get on those paths, she's going to have to change out of digital form.

The job of the **modem** is to translate digital information (numbers) into signals that can carry your message onto the Internet. The modem also works the other way. It translates signals back into digital code, too. So you don't have to miss your cousin's photos of her hamster's first birthday party.

Let's take a closer look at what happens when you get on the Web.

1. You open your Web browser, such as Safari or Internet Explorer. You type in a Web address. That address links to a set of files on a server out on the Internet somewhere. When you type it in, it's like you're asking the Internet, "Hey, can you find those files and send them to my computer?"

Can you find this on the Internet for me?

2. Next, your Internet Service Provider, or ISP, goes into action. This is the company, such as AT&T, that you (or your parents or school) pay each month to use the Internet. The ISP routes your request to a server.

3. The server searches. Does it have a match for the Web address? Routers send your request from server to server until a match is found. Yes! The server found a match.

4. Now the target server sends the files you asked for. But first, it breaks the files into packets. Each packet gets its own wrapper that tells where it came from, where it's going, and how to put it back together with the other packets.

5. Routers decide the fastest and easiest paths for each packet. By themselves, the packets can easily get around crowded or stalled areas. The complete file would likely get held up in those places.

6. Each packet is sent on its own merry way back to your device. It puts them back together, and . . . you've got your info!

CHAPTER FOUR

PLAY IT SAFE

Another way to think of the Internet is as an "information superhighway." There are no speed limits. No road signs. No police of any kind. This can be both exciting and dangerous. Think of your Internet experience like driving a car. You want to be sure to take the right turns and not get off at any unknown exits.

Somebody's probably already told you about the dangers of the Internet. One of them is misleading or bad information. A Web site might say that poison-tongued dart frogs live in shoeboxes. But you'd better check that at a better site before you put it in your school report. Some Web sites can lead you to scary or violent stuff for adults only. Creepy strangers who are looking to connect with kids for the wrong reasons might be lurking in kid chat rooms.

DON'T BULLY ME!

Cyberbullying is becoming a real problem at school and home. Some kids are using Facebook, YouTube, chat rooms, texts, and other electronic methods to bully other kids. They post untrue, embarrassing, or hurtful things about their victims. Nasty comments or lies can spread throughout the entire school in minutes.

Bullies who might not taunt a kid in person feel freer to do so over the Internet. According to one 2010 study, as many as one out of five US kids in middle school has been affected by this disturbing new trend.

What to Do

So, how can you play it safe when surfing the Internet? Here are some things to remember:

1. Never give your information to someone you don't know.
2. Don't answer e-mails from someone you don't know.
3. Stay on approved sites. If you don't know if they are approved, ask your parent or teacher.

4. Tell your parents or teacher right away if you notice anything suspicious.
5. Let a trusted adult know right away if you are the victim of cyberbullying.

Ask your parents if it's okay to check out a new Web site.

ATTACK!

A **virus** is a program that can infect your computer and make it "sick." Computer viruses can cause the information on your computer to download to another one. They can even wipe out all your stored memory or completely shut your computer down.

Viruses travel over the Internet. Some come from people who think viruses are a funny prank. Others might come from thieves looking to steal your parents' banking information.

How can you keep viruses from attacking? Be careful not to click on strange links or open an e-mail from someone you don't know. If you do get a virus, don't panic. The worst thing to do is to keep clicking on screens or pushing buttons. This can make it worse.

Your parent or teacher will probably run a program to help you to get rid of the virus safely.

I think I found your virus.

I feel worse.

CHAPTER FIVE

A NEW WAY TO CONNECT

The Internet has changed how we get information. No more standing in line at the bookstores. You can download an e-book on any topic within seconds. What will happen to actual bookstores? Some people predict they will soon be a thing of the past.

Many people use e-readers instead of reading books in hard copies.

Shakespeare
Sonnet 73

That time of year thou mayst in me behold
When yellow leaves, or none, or few do hang
Upon those boughs which shake against the cold
Bare ruined choirs where late the sweet birds sang.
In me thou seest the twilight of such day
As after sunset fadeth in the west,
Which by and by black night doth steal away,
Death's second self, which seals up all in rest.
In me thou seest the glowing of such fire
That on the ashes of his youth doth lie,
As the deathbed whereon it must expire,
Consumed with that which it was nourished by.
This thou perceiv'st, which makes thy love more strong,
To love that well which thou must leave ere long.

Sonnet CXXX.
"My mistress' eyes are nothing like the sun"

MY mistress' eyes are nothing like the sun
Coral is far more red than her lips' red:
If snow be white, why then her breasts are dun;
If hairs be wires, black wires grow on her head.
I have seen roses damask'd, red and white,
But no such roses see I in her cheeks;
And in some perfumes is there more delight
Than in the breath that from my mistress reeks.
I love to hear her speak, yet well I know
That music hath a far more pleasing sound:
I grant I never saw a goddess go,—
My mistress, when she walks, treads on the ground:
And yet, by heaven, I think my love as rare
As any she belied with false compare.

1   2   3   4   5
6   7   8   9   0

The Internet has also had a huge effect on newspapers—especially the paper version. More and more people are getting their news online. And now just about anybody—including you—can publish a blog. These electronic diaries are a favorite way to share views on school lunch, the president, your favorite song, the gum on the bottom of your shoe . . . whatever.

Today, people often read newspapers online.

TIME LINE

AROUND 300 BC
The library of Alexandria opens in Egypt. Considered the ancient world's greatest library, it is later burned down.

868 AD
The first book is printed in China.

1440
Gutenberg invents the printing press in Germany.

1600s
The first mechanical calculating machines are invented.

1837
Samuel Morse develops the telegraph system.

Sites on the Internet let people start blogs for free.

Some people are worried that traditional news organizations with trained journalists are dying off. They argue that blogs and other news sources are not reliable, and bad information spreads. Other people argue that the Internet is like a democracy. It lets everyone express their views—not just the experts. What do you think?

1854
The first free, US public library opens in Boston.

1946
The ENIAC is built. This house-sized machine is the world's first electronic, general-purpose computer.

1960
AT&T creates the very first modem.

LATE 1960s
ARPANET is created by the US Department of Defense.

1969
The first e-mail is sent.

SCHOOL.COM

The Internet is also changing how we go to school. Online schools are growing quickly. These schools range from first grade to college and offer degrees and certifications in hundreds of different areas. Could you imagine logging on to a computer to go to class? Many homeschoolers use online courses to add to what they're learning from their parents.

With online school, you can "attend" class from home.

1971
E-mail software is developed.

1975
The first personal computer, the Altair, is introduced.

1988
Chatting on the Internet becomes possible.

1991
The World Wide Web is created.

1996
The first wireless Internet service is offered by AT&T.

How Much Is Too Much?

What happens when you type more than you talk? Could it affect your social skills? Are kids spending as much quality time with their families and friends? What about the great outdoors—fresh air and exercise? Are video games turning your brain to mush? Experts are researching and debating all these possible harmful effects of the electronic age.

But wait a minute—while we're at it, let's consider some of the benefits of the Internet, too:

1. Great sites with up-to-date information on all your favorite topics from aardvarks to zombies.
2. Being able to keep in touch with friends and relatives around the world through e-mail, video chat, and more—and for free.

1996
Nokia introduces the first smartphone.

2004
Facebook is launched.

2005
YouTube is launched.

2007
Amazon releases an e-reader, the Kindle.

2010
The iPad arrives in US stores.

3. Fun games (educational ones, too).

4. Getting info on fun events that are happening right now in your city or town.

5. Researching a glow-in-the-dark microscope or other cool stuff that you might want to buy—and then buying it.

Most everybody agrees that balance is the key. Don't stay on the computer until your eyeballs are numb. If the computer is getting in the way of sleep, homework, sports, or family and friends, you know it's time to cut back.

What's Coming?

The Internet is constantly growing and changing. How will it change during the next 10, 30, or 50 years?

1. Faster, cheaper, bigger. As technology improves, the Internet is getting faster, and ISP fees keep going down. With 5 billion people yet to come online, the Internet can only get bigger.

2. More devices, fewer wires. Computers, phones, netbooks, MP3 players, tablets, TVs—the list of devices that get you on the Internet is growing, as are wireless networks. It's getting easier to get on the Web from anywhere.

3. Better graphics. If they haven't already, 3-D movies are coming to your device soon. Same with virtual reality. Someday when you chat online, you may feel as if your friend is right in the room with you.

WORDS TO KNOW

clients (KLY-uhnts): Clients are computers or devices that seek information from the Internet. Most devices on the Internet are clients.

modem (MOH-dehm): A modem is a device that converts digital information to signals that can travel over phone and cable lines. Most devices need a modem to connect to the Internet.

network (NEHT-wurk): A network is a system that links a group of computers. The Internet is a worldwide network.

routers (ROW-tuhrs): Routers are devices that send files from computer to computer along the Internet. Routers keep the flow of information organized on the Internet.

servers (SUR-vuhrs): Servers are computers that store information and send it to other computers. On the Internet, servers store and send the files that make up Web sites.

virus (VY-rus): A computer virus is a program that is secretly put into someone's computer through the Internet. A virus can destroy files and cause other problems for a computer.

FIND OUT MORE

Visit our Web site for links about how the Internet works:
childsworld.com/links

Note to Parents, Teachers, and Librarians: We routinely verify our Web links to make sure they are safe and active sites. So encourage your readers to check them out!

INDEX